Every

MW00881240

*A Rhyming Picture Book
for Kids Who Like to Giggle*

*Story and Illustrations
by Steve Hodge*

For information, contact:
stevehodge@mail.com

First Print Edition

NOTICE:

This story is **NOT** about a boy hanging upside-down in a tree with a bee on the end of his nose. In our story, there is no boy, there is no tree, there is no nose, there is no bee.

So try to forget the boy in a tree and his nose with a bee so that we can get on with our story.

Are you ready? Good! Let's begin.

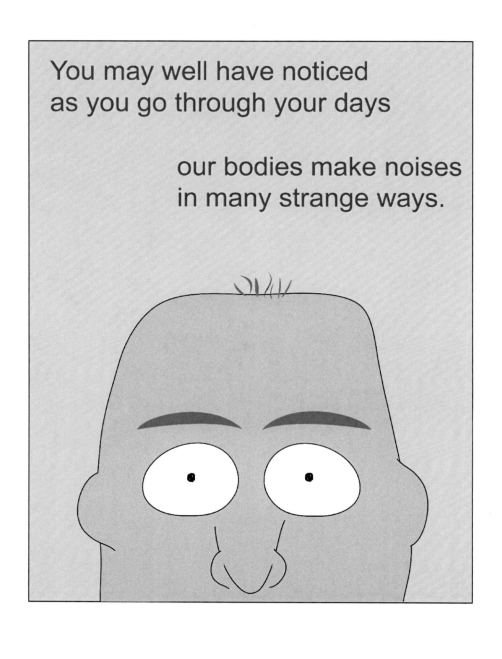

Sometimes in your kitchen,
or out on your lawn,
you'll open your mouth
and let out a big *yawn!*

When playing with toys,
while down on your knees,
you'll sometimes stop playing
to *ah-choo!* a big *sneeze!*

At the end of the day,

   as you're turning your light off,

   you're sometimes surprised

      when you *cough* a big *cough!*

You can hear your guts gurgle and the beating of your heart; your nose sometimes sniffles and sometimes ...

... you fart.

Don't think that you're awful
when gas comes from your fanny;
your father farts too
and so does your *granny!*

Your teacher,
the postman,
your best friend
and her brother
they all break wind
and *so does your mother!*

Kings, queens and paupers
who churn their own butter
are sometimes surprised
to feel their cheeks flutter

Queen Flatulence

You see, when you eat,
even food that tastes yummy,
your stomach makes gas
that gets trapped in your tummy.

The gas builds up in you,
but there it can't stay,
so sometimes you burp
or it goes out the other way.

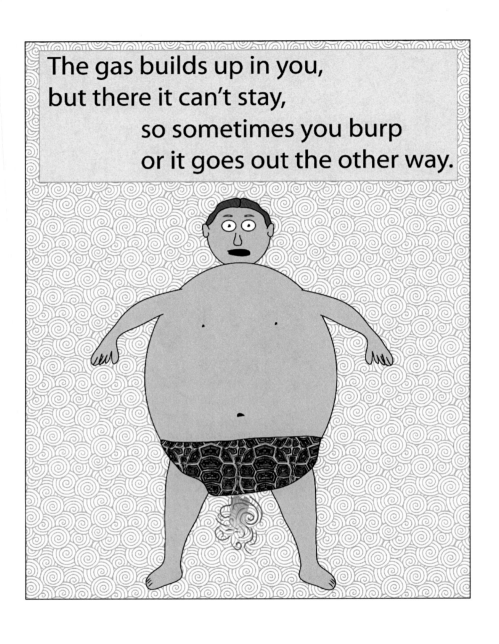

It's okay to perform one
when alone in your room ...

If you pass gas in bed

you can think you're a winner ...

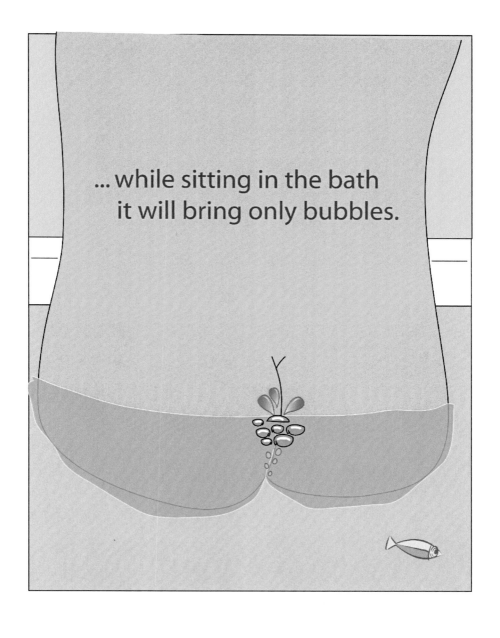

... while sitting in the bath
it will bring only bubbles.

They often bring laughter,
sometimes they bring sorrow
but one thing's for sure;
you'll make more tomorrow.

But wait!
There's more!

Hello again!

I've been thinking about the boy hanging upside-down in a tree with a bee on the end of his nose. It doesn't seem right to just leave him there. Can you make up a story about a boy in a tree and his nose with a bee?

Why don't you try? It might be great fun!

Until next time; good-bye!

Also by Steve Hodge

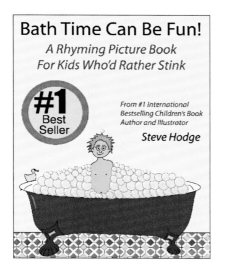

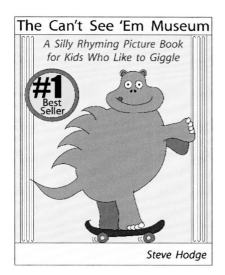

Find even more of Steve's children's books online

About the Author

A former educator and graduate of the San Francisco Art Institute, Steve Hodge's rhyming picture books have entertained thousands of children all around the world and helped guide countless kids onto the path toward learning to read.

Many of Steve's books became #1 bestsellers within days of their publication and several were chosen #1 "Hot New Release" the months they were published.

Visit Steve's blog to learn more about him, see new drawings for his upcoming books, try to guess the answers to his riddles and have some fun!

Steve's blog can be found at:

http://stevehodgeblog.blogspot.com

29236458R00018

Made in the USA
Middletown, DE
11 February 2016